MONSTERS & MYTHS
DRAGONS AND SERPENTS

By Gerrie McCall and Lisa Regan

Gareth Stevens
Publishing

Please visit our Web site, www.garethstevens.com. For a free color catalog of all our high-quality books, call toll free 1-800-542-2595 or fax 1-877-542-2596.

Library of Congress Cataloging-in-Publication Data

McCall, Gerrie.
 Dragons and serpents / Gerrie McCall and Lisa Regan.
    p. cm. — (Monsters & myths)
 Includes index.
 ISBN 978-1-4339-4997-5 (library binding)
 ISBN 978-1-4339-4998-2 (pbk.)
 ISBN 978-1-4339-4999-9 (6-pack)
 1. Dragons. 2. Serpents. I. Regan, Lisa. II. Title.
 GR830.D7M38 2011
 398.24'54–dc22
                                    2010033446

Published in 2011 by
Gareth Stevens Publishing
111 East 14th Street, Suite 349
New York, NY 10003

Copyright © 2011 Amber Books Ltd, London

Illustrations copyright © Amber Books and IMP AB

Printed in the United States of America

CPSIA compliance information: Batch #CW11GS: For further information contact Gareth Stevens, New York, New York at 1-800-542-2595.

Table of Contents

Fafnir

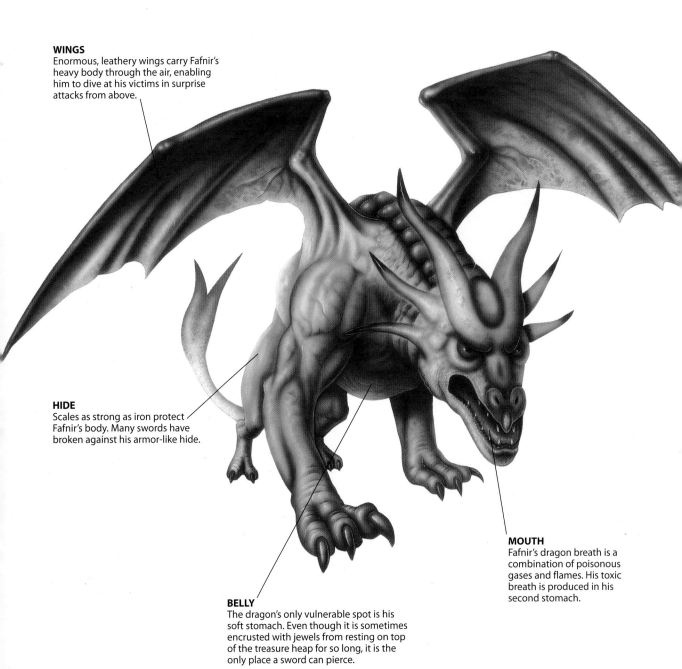

WINGS
Enormous, leathery wings carry Fafnir's heavy body through the air, enabling him to dive at his victims in surprise attacks from above.

HIDE
Scales as strong as iron protect Fafnir's body. Many swords have broken against his armor-like hide.

MOUTH
Fafnir's dragon breath is a combination of poisonous gases and flames. His toxic breath is produced in his second stomach.

BELLY
The dragon's only vulnerable spot is his soft stomach. Even though it is sometimes encrusted with jewels from resting on top of the treasure heap for so long, it is the only place a sword can pierce.

Fafnir is a simple dwarf warped by greed. Fafnir and his brother Regin want a share of their father's treasure. Fafnir murders his father for the treasure and refuses to share with Regin. Years of gloating over his treasure transform Fafnir from a dwarf into a terrible dragon. Still hungry for a share of the treasure, Regin asks the hero Sigurd to slay Fafnir. The hero needs a reliable sword because the dragon's scales are impenetrable. Sigurd repairs his father's broken sword, making it unbreakable and sturdy enough to split an anvil.

Sigurd digs a trench across the path Fafnir follows for his daily drink at the river. Hidden in the trench, Sigurd thrusts his mighty sword into Fafnir's belly as he slithers overhead. At Regin's request, Sigurd cuts out Fafnir's heart and roasts it. Sigurd burns his fingers on the red-hot heart. When he sucks on his fingers to relieve the pain, the taste of Fafnir's blood gives Sigurd the power to understand the language of birds. The birds warn Sigurd that Regin plans to kill him, so Sigurd kills Regin and claims the treasure.

ACTUAL SIZE

WHERE IN THE WORLD?

NORWAY

According to Norse mythology, Fafnir crouches atop his heap of hoarded treasure in a cold, dark Norwegian cave.

DID YOU KNOW?

• Until Sigurd came along, Fafnir was thought to be undefeatable. Numerous brave men went seeking the dragon's treasure but were burned alive and eaten.

• Fafnir's father was the king of dwarf folk. Several Norse gods gave Fafnir's father treasure as payment for accidentally killing one of Fafnir's brothers.

• The sword that Sigurd has repaired in order to slay Fafnir was once his father's. It broke when his father battled Odin, the chief god in Norse mythology. As his father lay dying, he predicted that his unborn son would one day forge a powerful weapon from the fragments of his broken sword.

Futs-Lung

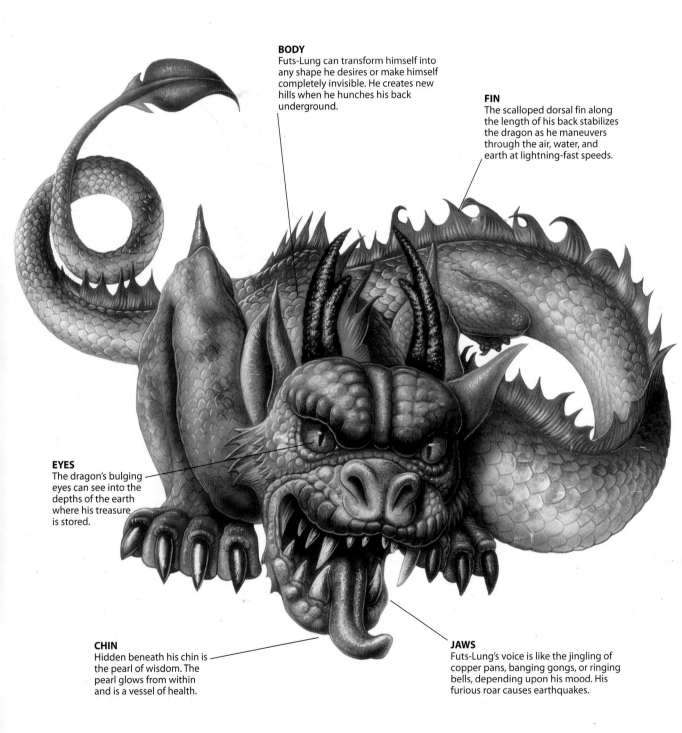

BODY
Futs-Lung can transform himself into any shape he desires or make himself completely invisible. He creates new hills when he hunches his back underground.

FIN
The scalloped dorsal fin along the length of his back stabilizes the dragon as he maneuvers through the air, water, and earth at lightning-fast speeds.

EYES
The dragon's bulging eyes can see into the depths of the earth where his treasure is stored.

CHIN
Hidden beneath his chin is the pearl of wisdom. The pearl glows from within and is a vessel of health.

JAWS
Futs-Lung's voice is like the jingling of copper pans, banging gongs, or ringing bells, depending upon his mood. His furious roar causes earthquakes.

The dragon of hidden treasures that lives deep within the Earth is Futs-Lung. He guards all the precious gems and priceless metals in his lair. Futs-Lung possesses a magic pearl that multiplies when touched, which represents wisdom. It took 3,000 years for Futs-Lung to grow to his terrific adult size. Newly hatched, he looked much like an eel. By 500 years of age, Futs-Lung had grown a head that resembles a carp's. By his 1,500th birthday, he will have a long tail, a head with a thick beard, and four stumpy legs with claws. At the age of 2,000, Futs-Lung will have horns.

In modern-day Hong Kong, there is an apartment complex that was built near a mountain where Futs-Lung lives. The complex was designed with a large gap in the middle so that Futs-Lung's ocean view would remain unobstructed and his goodwill would be maintained. Like most Chinese dragons, Futs-Lung is benevolent until offended. His wrath should not be roused. He must be treated with respect and reverence so he does not unleash his incredible temper. Volcanoes are formed when Futs-Lung bursts from the earth and reports to heaven.

ACTUAL SIZE

WHERE IN THE WORLD?

CHINA

Futs-Lung is the underworld dragon of China. He is in charge of guarding all the precious metals and gems buried in the Earth.

DID YOU KNOW?

• Imperial Chinese dragons have five toes, Korean dragons four, and Japanese dragons three.

• Chinese dragons lay one egg at a time. Each dragon egg takes 1,000 years to hatch.

• The Chinese refer to themselves as "descendants of the dragon."

• Chinese dragons have 117 scales on their serpentine bodies.

• It was a compliment to refer to someone as "dragon face" in China. Many founding emperors of dynasties were described as having dragon faces. It was considered a lucky sign indicating their future greatness.

• Chinese dragons are shape shifters that can change into the form of a man, shrink themselves down to a mouse, or expand until they fill up the space between heaven and Earth.

Gorynych

HEADS
Three fanged, fire-spitting heads with terrible horns make it impossible to approach Gorynych. Six watchful eyes and a heightened sense of smell enable him to detect a maiden from a mile (1.6 km) away.

BODY
The scaly body produces a reek of sulfur that hangs around Gorynych like a sinister cloud.

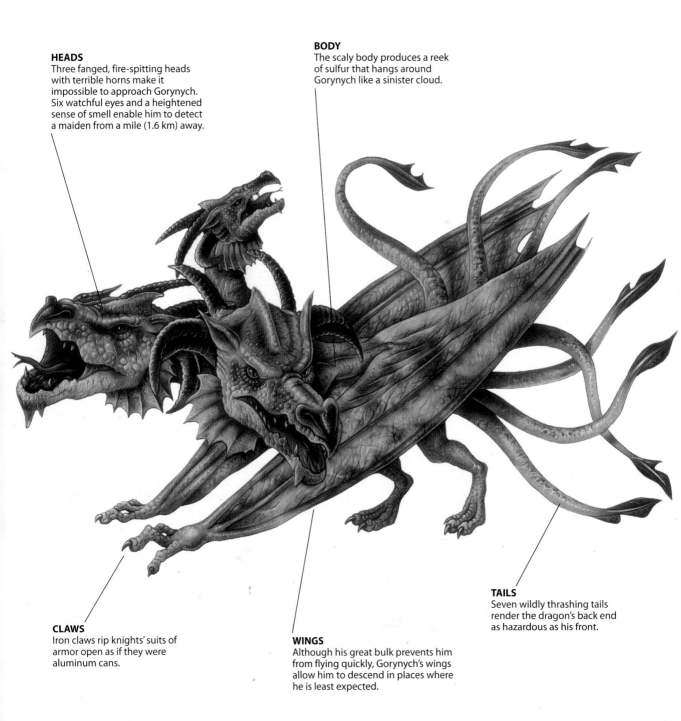

CLAWS
Iron claws rip knights' suits of armor open as if they were aluminum cans.

WINGS
Although his great bulk prevents him from flying quickly, Gorynych's wings allow him to descend in places where he is least expected.

TAILS
Seven wildly thrashing tails render the dragon's back end as hazardous as his front.

This savage Russian dragon has three fire-spitting heads and seven tails. Gorynych walks on his two hind legs and has two small front legs like a *Tyrannosaurus rex*. His iron claws can slash through any shield or suit of armor. The air around Gorynych reeks of sulfur, a sign of its evil. His uncle, the sorcerer Nemal Chelovek, kidnaps the czar's daughter and intends for her to wed Gorynych. The princess is imprisoned in the sorcerer's dark mountain castle. Desperate to have his daughter back, the czar offers a huge reward to anyone who can rescue the princess from the castle. Many princes try and fail.

ACTUAL SIZE

Ivan, a palace guard who understands the speech of animals, overhears two crows discussing where the princess is hidden. The czar gives Ivan a magic sword to help him on his rescue mission. Nemal Chelovek's fortress is unguarded because he believes no one would dare approach him. Nemal Chelovek turns himself into a giant when he discovers Ivan in his castle. The magic sword flies from Ivan's hands, killing the giant, then flies through the castle halls until it finds and slays Gorynych. Ivan marries the princess.

WHERE IN THE WORLD?

- RUSSIA
- UKRAINE

The fearsome seven-tailed Gorynych is featured in folktales and myths originating from Russia and Ukraine.

DID YOU KNOW?

• Gorynych caused eclipses of the sun and moon. The fact that they reappeared showed that even a powerful dragon could not defeat the sun and moon. The Russians took this as a sign that dragons can be defeated by the righteous.

• Not all Slavic dragons are destructive. The Slovenian city of Ljubljana is protected by a dragon. This benevolent dragon is pictured on the city's coat of arms.

• Dragon blood is so venomous that the Earth does not absorb it.

• There are no cave paintings of dragons because caves are a favorite residence of dragons. The dragon residing in the cave would have driven all cave painters away.

• A magic sword that enables the warrior to stand far away from the dragon is the ideal weapon for battle with dragons.

Hatuibwari

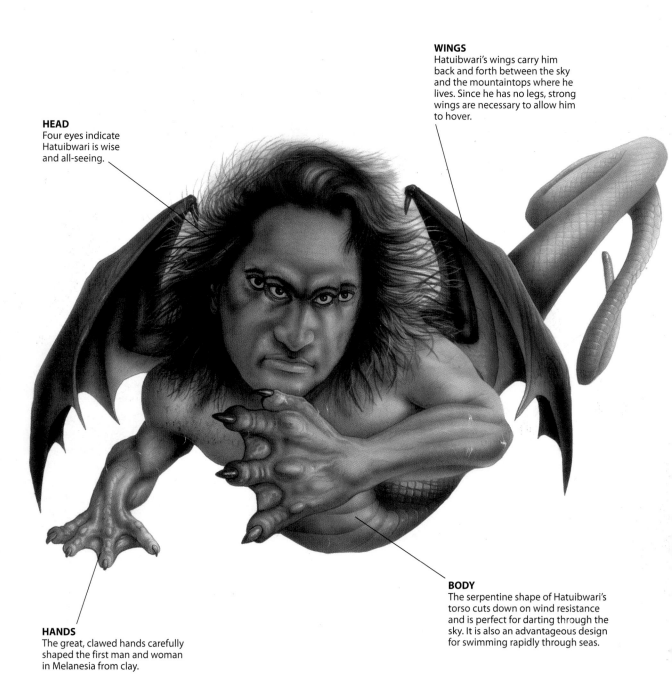

WINGS
Hatuibwari's wings carry him back and forth between the sky and the mountaintops where he lives. Since he has no legs, strong wings are necessary to allow him to hover.

HEAD
Four eyes indicate Hatuibwari is wise and all-seeing.

HANDS
The great, clawed hands carefully shaped the first man and woman in Melanesia from clay.

BODY
The serpentine shape of Hatuibwari's torso cuts down on wind resistance and is perfect for darting through the sky. It is also an advantageous design for swimming rapidly through seas.

On San Cristobal Island in Melanesia, the ancient belief is that the dragon Hatuibwari created and nourished all living things. He is the male version of Mother Earth, with a body that is half human and half snake. Two enormous wings carry him through the skies and four eyes allow him to see everything under the sun. Hatuibwari rolls red clay in his hands, breathes on it, and forms the shape of a human. He places the clay figure in the sun and it comes to life as the first woman. Later, while the first woman is asleep, Hatuibwari takes a rib from her side, adds more clay, and creates the first man.

ACTUAL SIZE

One day Hatuibwari coils around his human grandson to comfort him. The child's father comes home and mistakes Hatuibwari for an enormous serpent squeezing the life from his child. The frightened father does not recognize the dragon spirit as his father-in-law and cuts Hatuibwari to pieces with a knife. The pieces unite again at once. Angry and offended, Hatuibwari announces that he is leaving and will cause the people's crops to fail. Hatuibwari departs to live on Guadalcanal Island and everything deteriorates in his absence.

WHERE IN THE WORLD?

SOLOMON ISLANDS

Hatuibwari lives in the sky and on sacred mountaintops of San Cristobal and Guadalcanal in the Solomon Islands, Melanesia.

DID YOU KNOW?

• **Hatuibwari often appears in a sacred grove. Anyone who does not treat the grove with proper reverence and respect is stricken with illness and terrible sores.**

• **Sacrifices of pigs are offered to Hatuibwari to appease him. Like Chinese and Japanese dragons, he must be treated with respect or he will grow angry.**

• **Hatuibwari causes rains to fall in order to quench his thirst.**

• **Babylonian, Chinese, Australian, and Aztec mythologies all contain stories of dragons as creators of life on Earth.**

• **In Melanesian mythology, darkness, forever, and the sea have always existed. Hatuibwari created animals, food, trees, and humans. He travels between our world and the sky.**

Hungarian Horntail

TAIL
A whip of the spike-lined tail easily kills the dragon's enemies. When angered, the thrashing tail rips up large patches of sod.

HEAD
The terrible head bears bronze horns used to gore its victims. Its hearing is so acute that the dragon can detect any approaching threat from a great distance away.

JAWS
When not producing a yowling, screeching scream that curdles the blood, the jaws emit a stream of fire that reaches as far as 50 feet (15 m).

CLAWS
Sharp, curved claws slash at the flesh of enemies or grip its victim's body as the dragon's fangs carry out their gruesome work.

EYES
The yellow eyes contain a reflective layer that enables the dragon to detect things five times more effectively than a human can.

As the first task of the Triwizard Tournament in J.K. Rowling's *Harry Potter and the Goblet of Fire,* Harry must get past a mother Hungarian Horntail and steal a golden egg from her nest. The golden egg is placed among her clutch of gray eggs. A nesting mother Horntail is especially hazardous when defending her young. Harry summons his racing broom and uses it to fly back and forth, taunting the dragon. He dodges blasts of fire deftly on his broom, but has one shoulder scraped by her thrashing, spiked tail. He lures the furious dragon up onto her hind legs by flying high above her, then swoops down and snatches the golden egg.

The Hungarian Horntail is remarkably dangerous because it can do as much damage with its spike-lined tail as it can with its fanged mouth, which shoots jets of fire up to a distance of 50 feet (15 m). The young use their spiked tails to club their way out of their eggs. It can require anywhere from 6 to 8 well-trained wizards to subdue a fully grown Hungarian Horntail with stunning spells. It is considered the most dangerous of all dragon breeds, according to the Ministry of Magic.

ACTUAL SIZE

WHERE IN THE WORLD?

HUNGARY

Normally native to Hungary, smuggling of the Hungarian Horntail's eggs has led to sightings of the dragon in England.

DID YOU KNOW?

• **The blood, heart, horn, hide, and liver of dragons all have magical properties.**

• **There are 10 breeds of purebred dragon that can interbreed and produce hybrid dragons.**

• **The female dragon is larger and more aggressive than the male dragon.**

• **The motto for Hogwarts School of Witchcraft and Wizardry—*Draco Dormiens Nunquam Titillandus*— means "Never tickle a sleeping dragon."**

• **The dinosaur *Dracorex Hogwartsia*, which means "dragon king of Hogwarts," was named by young visitors to the Children's Museum of Indianapolis.**

• **The Ministry of Magic has classified the Hungarian Horntail as a known wizard killer.**

DRAGONS AND SERPENTS

Jawzahr

HEAD
Jawzahr's huge, horned head is able to live independently from his body. His eyes glint with perpetual malice.

TAIL
A spade-shaped tuft at the end of his tail indicates Jawzahr is a male. Female dragons lack this tuft.

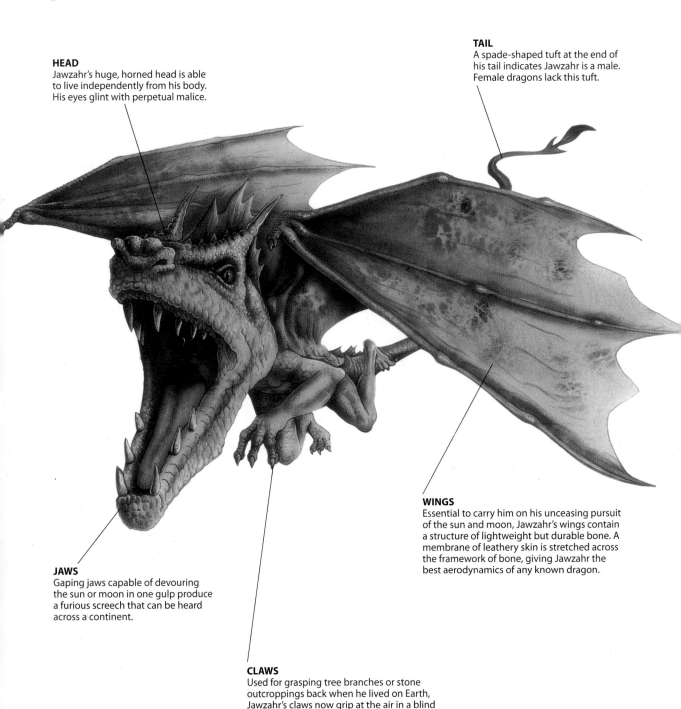

JAWS
Gaping jaws capable of devouring the sun or moon in one gulp produce a furious screech that can be heard across a continent.

WINGS
Essential to carry him on his unceasing pursuit of the sun and moon, Jawzahr's wings contain a structure of lightweight but durable bone. A membrane of leathery skin is stretched across the framework of bone, giving Jawzahr the best aerodynamics of any known dragon.

CLAWS
Used for grasping tree branches or stone outcroppings back when he lived on Earth, Jawzahr's claws now grip at the air in a blind rage as he flies through the night skies.

In ancient Persia, eclipses occur when Jawzahr the comet dragon swallows the sun or moon. He menaces the two great luminaries, chasing them around the sky and devouring them at regular intervals. Jawzahr is a crafty, curious dragon. He disguises himself as a god and drinks an immortality-giving potion meant only for the gods. The sun and moon, however, see everything and they report Jawzahr's trickery to the gods. As punishment, Jawzahr's head is severed with one well aimed throw of a discus. But Jawzahr is already immortal because of the potion he drank, and cannot be killed.

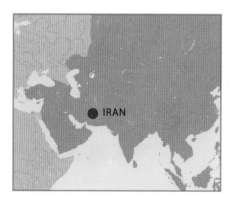

ACTUAL SIZE

Enraged, Jawzahr ascends to the sky. The two immortal parts of him live on separate from each other. Jawzahr is angry at both the sun and moon for revealing his deception to the gods. He forever chases the sun and moon, gobbling them down when he catches them. Any time an eclipse occurs, it means that Jawzahr has caught up with and consumed the sun or the moon. As for his tail, it emits a shower of comets that stream across the night sky.

WHERE IN THE WORLD?

IRAN

A dragon from Islamic mythology, Jawzahr first made his appearance in legends from Persia, which is modern-day Iran.

DID YOU KNOW?

• The astronomical location of the dragon's head and dragon's tail mark the points where solar and lunar eclipses may occur.

• Draco, a constellation in the northern hemisphere, gets its name from the Latin word for dragon. One of the brightest stars in Draco is in its tail and is named Thuban, which is the Arabic word for dragon. About 5,000 years ago Thuban was the Pole Star, Earth's North Star. The ancient Egyptians recognized Thuban as the North Star at the time they were constructing the Great Pyramid. Today the North Star is Polaris.

• Many ancient cultures believed that comets were dragons streaking across the sky.

• Another star in Draco is Rastaban, which means "head of the dragon."

Jormungand

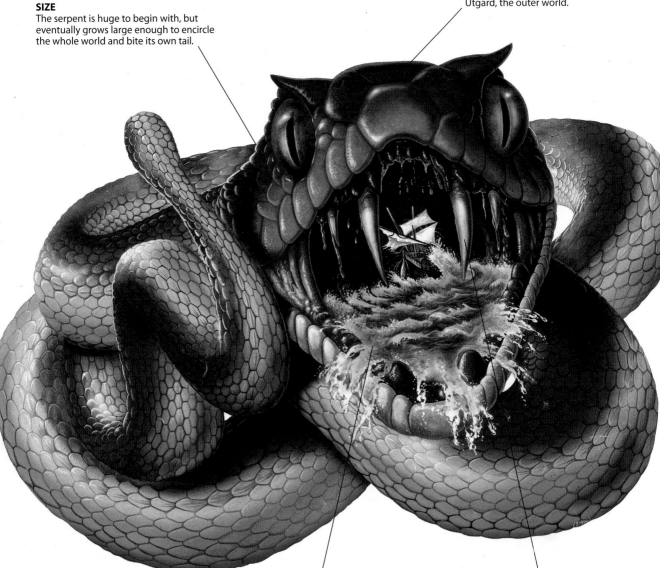

TRICKERY
Thor is tricked into thinking that Jormungand is a cat that must be lifted as one of Thor's tasks in Utgard, the outer world.

SIZE
The serpent is huge to begin with, but eventually grows large enough to encircle the whole world and bite its own tail.

VENOM
His venom is so powerful that at the end of the world, it will destroy all life on Earth, and kill Thor before he can take nine steps.

FANGS
Jormungand's mighty fangs are as sharp as daggers and used to inject a lethal venom.

In the Norse myths of Scandinavia, Jormungand is the "world serpent" or Midgard Serpent. Midgard is one of nine worlds in these myths and is the home of humankind. It is surrounded by an ocean that is bigger than any world and cannot be crossed, and this is where the serpent Jormungand eventually makes its home. Jormungand is an evil being and the main enemy of Thor, the god of thunder. At the end of the world, called Ragnarok (the doom of the gods), Jormungand will rear up and lash the land with waves, poisoning the land, sky, and ocean, and killing Thor with its venom.

The trickster god Loki and his giantess wife, Angrboda, had three children: Jormungand, Hel, and Fenrir. At a very young age, it became clear that the serpent Jormungand would cause problems with its size and its evil, poisonous ways. So Odin, the chief of the gods, sent a group to catch the serpent and throw it into the ocean. There it grew big enough to encircle the Earth so that all of mankind was caught in its coils. At the end of time, the serpent will escape and spew his venom everywhere.

CIRCLES WORLD

WHERE IN THE WORLD?

SCANDINAVIA

The Norse myths come from many northern European countries, especially Scandinavia (Denmark, Sweden, Norway, and Iceland).

DID YOU KNOW?

• Several ancient cultures have a symbol showing a serpent or dragon swallowing its own tail and forming a circle. It is known as the Ouroboros and is important for showing the cyclical nature of things.

• Jormungand's younger sister Hel is half alive and half dead. His older brother Fenrir is a wolf.

• All of Loki's children were seen as problems for the gods. Hel was banished to the underworld, and Fenrir was bound to a rock by magical chains.

• Thor meets Jormungand at least three times: when he is tricked by the cat illusion, when he goes fishing with the giant Hymir to catch the serpent using an ox head as bait, and at Ragnarok, the end of time.

Knucker

TAIL
Capable of swatting down trees, the gigantic tail is the dragon's most dangerous appendage.

EYES
Eerie eyes glow with a chemical that allows the Knucker to see great distances in the densest waters and on land.

JAWS
Immense jaws open wide enough to swallow a horse and cart whole. Teeth larger than railroad spikes line a mouth that reeks of the Knucker's nauseating breath.

BODY
A streamlined, eel-shaped body aids the Knucker in navigating quickly and silently through the chilly waters of the knuckerhole.

WINGS
Small wings allow the Knucker to fly low through marshy areas in search of likely victims. When in water, the wings act as fins.

A terrible, water-dwelling dragon, the Knucker makes nightly raids on Lyminster farms for meals of horses and cows. Any person crossing its path is just another meal to the Knucker. The dragon squeezes its prey to death or shreds its victim's flesh to ribbons with its poisonous fangs. Many a still night in Lyminster is shattered by the hiss and roar of the ravenous dragon. So many villagers and farm animals go missing that the mayor offers a reward to anyone who can kill the Knucker and allow the villagers to live without fear.

ACTUAL SIZE

Jim, a farmer's boy from a nearby village, tells the mayor his plan to defeat the Knucker. The mayor orders the villagers to help Jim with everything he needs. The villagers give Jim all the ingredients for an enormous pie. Jim bakes a gigantic pie laced with poison for the Knucker. He hauls the pie out to the knuckerhole using a borrowed cart and horse. The Knucker eats the pie, horse, and cart. The poison kills the dreaded dragon and Jim chops off its head with an ax.

WHERE IN THE WORLD?

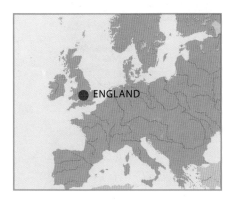

ENGLAND

The Knucker rises from the knuckerhole in Lyminster, West Sussex. Its residence, the knuckerhole, is a bottomless pool fed by an underground spring.

DID YOU KNOW?

• St. Mary Magdalene Church in Lyminster contains the Slayer's Slab, a gravestone dedicated to the hero who killed the Knucker.

• The British explorer Sir Francis Drake was called "The Dragon" by the Spanish because he was a fierce warrior and he helped defeat the Spanish Armada.

• The knuckerhole where the Knucker lives is a bottomless pool that neither freezes in winter nor dries up in summer. Six bell ropes from Lyminster Church were tied together and let down in the knuckerhole to measure its depth, but the bottom was never found.

• Residents of Lyminster once used water from the knuckerhole as a cure-all tonic.

• The county of Sussex once had a thriving dragon population. Bignor Hill and St. Leonard's Forest in Sussex also have a history of dragon infestations.

Krak's Dragon

TAIL
The swishing tail knocks over fences, damages bridge supports, and strips bark from trees. It can also crush a human's rib cage with a single blow.

HEAD
The dragon's massive skull is counterbalanced in flight by its long tail. Its piercing vision allows it to spot its next meal from half a mile (0.8 km) away.

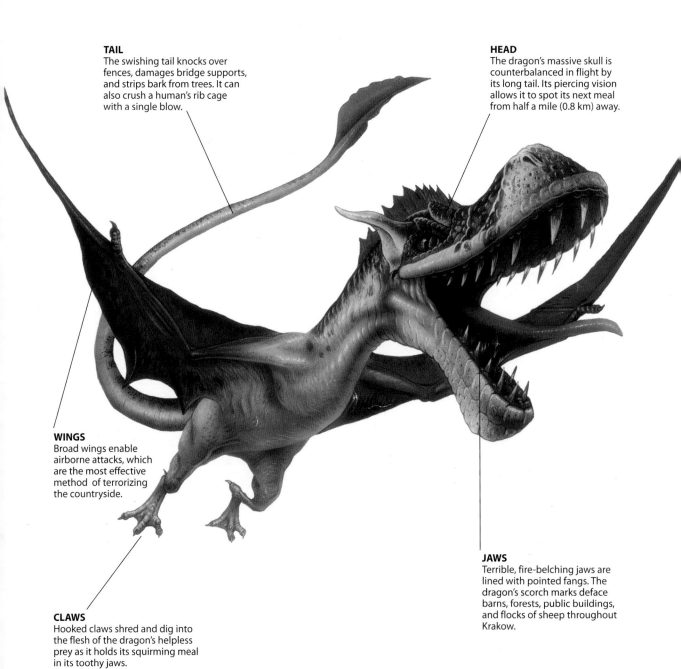

WINGS
Broad wings enable airborne attacks, which are the most effective method of terrorizing the countryside.

JAWS
Terrible, fire-belching jaws are lined with pointed fangs. The dragon's scorch marks deface barns, forests, public buildings, and flocks of sheep throughout Krakow.

CLAWS
Hooked claws shred and dig into the flesh of the dragon's helpless prey as it holds its squirming meal in its toothy jaws.

In Polish legend, a fearsome dragon lives in a dark cave at the foot of Wawel Hill along the banks of the Vistula River. Every day it rages through the countryside, terrifying the inhabitants of Krakow. The bad-tempered, fire-breathing dragon eats farm animals and people. Anything that runs from it is fair game. After it gobbles down several small children, it plunders homes for prized possessions to take back to its cave. Many bold knights try to slay this dragon and perish in flame for their efforts. Its daily thefts begin to affect the local economy. The people of the area grow poorer and the princess worries she will never marry.

Krak, a peasant boy employed as a shoemaker's apprentice, is intelligent, cunning, and has unique culinary skills. The king is desperate for anyone's dragon-slaying services and allows the raggedly dressed boy to try. Krak stuffs three roasted sheep full of sulfur and hot spices and leaves the spicy meal next to the dragon's cave. The greedy dragon gulps them down whole. The spices and sulfur burn the dragon's stomach. It drinks half the Vistula River to quench its thirst. Its swollen, burning gut bursts and kills it.

ACTUAL
SIZE

DID YOU KNOW?

• **The city of Krakow is named after the heroic Krak.**

• **Near the cavern beneath the castle of Krakow, there is a monument to Krak's dragon. The statue of the dragon has been rigged with a natural-gas nozzle so that it breathes fire every few minutes.**

• **Krak marries the princess and is given the dragon's hoarded treasure. After the death of the king, Krak ascends the throne.**

• **Many dragons prefer to sleep on top of a pile of jewels and treasure because more traditional bedding materials are too easily ignited by their fiery breath.**

• **Trickery is often the preferred method for defeating the most dangerous dragons. Cunning is generally a mightier weapon than a sword when facing a beast of such tremendous size, aggression, and appetite.**

WHERE IN THE WORLD?

● POLAND

Every citizen of Poland is familiar with the stories of the death, trauma, and destruction caused by Krak's dragon.

Kraken

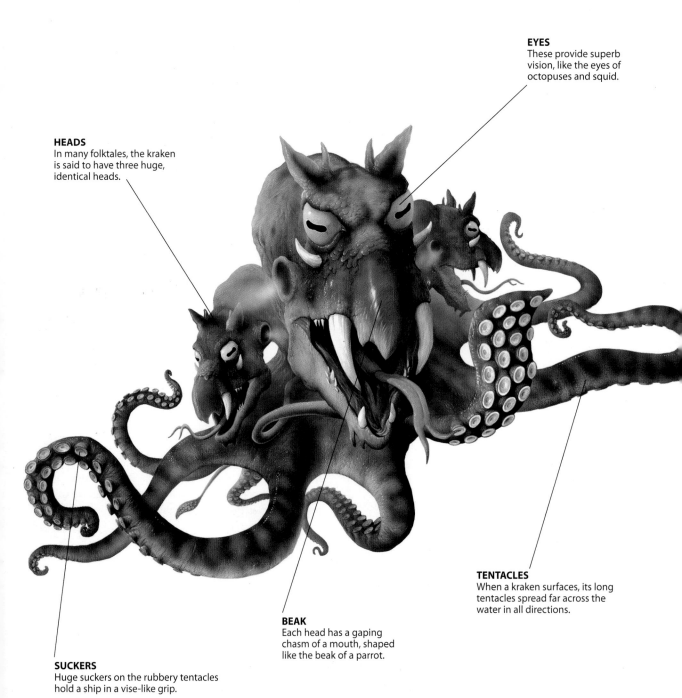

EYES
These provide superb vision, like the eyes of octopuses and squid.

HEADS
In many folktales, the kraken is said to have three huge, identical heads.

TENTACLES
When a kraken surfaces, its long tentacles spread far across the water in all directions.

BEAK
Each head has a gaping chasm of a mouth, shaped like the beak of a parrot.

SUCKERS
Huge suckers on the rubbery tentacles hold a ship in a vise-like grip.

Since medieval times, sailors and fishermen from western Europe—especially Scandinavia—have told of a vast, tentacled sea monster that lives in the ocean depths. The kraken is a mountain of a creature, dwarfing the largest of whales. In one book on the natural history of Norway, published in 1754, the Bishop of Bergen even claimed that the monster's body was almost 1.5 miles (2.5 km) in circumference.

ACTUAL
SIZE

← 0.6 MILES (1 KM) →

In the seas off northern Europe, a travel-weary captain sights land at last. His charts make no reference to the strangely rounded islands, but he trusts his eyes and steers his ship toward them. As he draws closer, the captain realizes his mistake with horror. The "islands" erupt from the sea to reveal a huge kraken. The waking monster seizes the ship in a mighty tentacle and plunges it beneath the boiling waves. Grasping one of the crew, it lifts him, screaming, into a gaping beak.

WHERE IN THE WORLD?

● NORWAY

Most of the legends tell us the kraken lived around the coasts of Scandinavia, especially in the deep waters off Norway. But similar tales also come from other coastal areas of Europe.

DID YOU KNOW?

• In some tales, the kraken has 1,000 tentacles and 10 mouths.

• There are reports of accidental kraken strandings. In 1680, a young kraken supposedly died after it was caught on the reefs off Alstadhang in Norway. And in 1775, another was found on the Isle of Bute in Scotland.

• The English 19th-century poet Alfred Lord Tennyson wrote a poem, "The Kraken," inspired by the myths.

Ladon

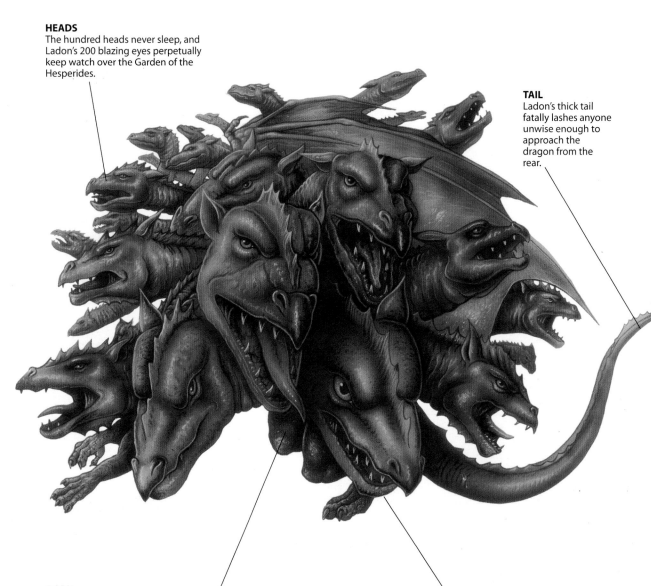

HEADS
The hundred heads never sleep, and Ladon's 200 blazing eyes perpetually keep watch over the Garden of the Hesperides.

TAIL
Ladon's thick tail fatally lashes anyone unwise enough to approach the dragon from the rear.

BODY
Ladon's muscular, serpentine body has a grip so tight that no mortal can pry him off. He tortures his victims by squeezing the life out of them, slowly suffocating them in his coils.

JAWS
Each one of the awful heads speaks in a different voice from jaws lined with teeth as sharp as knives.

In Greek mythology, Ladon is a monstrous dragon with 100 heads who twines his serpentine body around a tree bearing golden apples. He was placed in the Garden of the Hesperides by Hera, queen of the Olympians, to guard the garden and its golden apples. Not one of Ladon's hundred heads ever sleeps and each head speaks with a different voice. Ladon's 200 fiery, watchful eyes ensure that no one approaches the apples. Anyone who dares to sail to the ends of the earth in search of Hera's golden apples risks being torn to pieces.

 The King of Mycenae tests Hercules by assigning him 12 labors. The eleventh labor requires Hercules to steal the golden apples that Ladon guards. Hercules dips his arrow tips in the blood of a hydra and fires the poisoned arrows over the garden wall at Ladon. The awful dragon is felled by the poisoned arrows, and Hercules enters the garden safely. He steals the apples and completes his eleventh labor. Passing sailors later report having seen the slain Ladon with only the tip of his tail still twitching.

ACTUAL SIZE

WHERE IN THE WORLD?

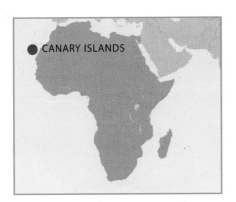

CANARY ISLANDS

The Garden of the Hesperides, where Ladon winds around the tree of golden apples, lies in the Canary Islands off the coast of Africa, not far from Mount Atlas.

DID YOU KNOW?

• After his death, Hera places Ladon in the sky as the constellation Draco, where he snakes around the North Pole eternally.

• The Latin word for a dragon, *draco*, means snake or serpent.

• Where blood from Ladon's wounds drenched the ground, dragon trees sprouted from each drop. Dragon trees have massive trunks and twisted branches. Their sap, called "dragon tree blood," is dark red and is believed to have healing properties.

• Direct frontal attack is the least effective way to slay a dragon. Hercules is wise enough to maintain a safe distance from the beast and use the stout garden wall as a shield.

Lambton Worm

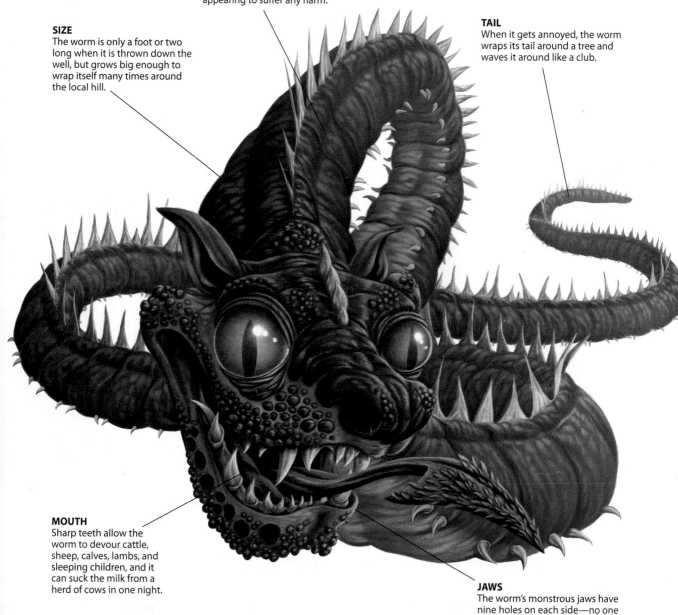

BODY
No matter how many times the worm is cut into pieces, it can join its parts back together without appearing to suffer any harm.

TAIL
When it gets annoyed, the worm wraps its tail around a tree and waves it around like a club.

SIZE
The worm is only a foot or two long when it is thrown down the well, but grows big enough to wrap itself many times around the local hill.

MOUTH
Sharp teeth allow the worm to devour cattle, sheep, calves, lambs, and sleeping children, and it can suck the milk from a herd of cows in one night.

JAWS
The worm's monstrous jaws have nine holes on each side—no one seems to know what purpose they serve.

This vast magical serpent grew from small but doomed beginnings. It was caught in the Wear River, near Lambton Castle, by the young lord himself. Seeing that it was a strange, ugly, evil-looking creature, he threw it down a nearby well. Many years passed, and the young lord served his country in the Crusades. During the time he was away, the worm grew and grew, and eventually crawled out of the well to strike terror through the land. It ate their farm animals and stole their children from their beds at night. No matter how they tried to defeat it, it could not be destroyed.

The Lord of Lambton returned and knew that he must save the people from this horrific curse. He asked a local witch what to do. Following her advice, he had a suit of armor made that was studded with spear blades. He stood on a rock in the middle of the raging river, and challenged the worm. Every time he sliced off its tail, the waters carried it away. The worm grew so angry that it coiled around him, to squeeze him to death, but instead it slashed itself into many pieces on the blades of his armor.

ACTUAL SIZE

WHERE IN THE WORLD?

NORTHUMBRIA

Tales of the worm are told in Northumbria in the northeast of England.

DID YOU KNOW?

• The story has a sad ending: the witch warns the Lord that to pay for her advice, he must kill the first creature he sees after the worm is defeated. Unfortunately, his father runs up to congratulate him, and he knows he must kill his father or be cursed once more.

• The curse says that nine generations of Lambtons will not die peacefully in their bed. This came true for the first three generations who died in battle or were drowned.

• Several songs and plays have been written about the Lambton worm, and are still performed today in England's northeast.

Luckdragon

EYES
Eyes glow in the luckdragon's noble head. He is able to spot landmarks far below him on the ground even when traveling through the clouds at top speed.

BACK
Falkor's enormous back accommodates heroes who need to be carried through the air on important quests.

JAWS
Falkor's lion-like mouth produces blue flame. The luckdragon is the only dragon known to spew blue fire. His song sounds like the golden note of a large bell.

BODY
The long, graceful body with pearl-colored scales requires no wings for soaring. The luckdragon uses levitation for flight rather than traditional dragon wings.

A dragon species in Michael Ende's novel *The Neverending Story*, the luckdragon is a wingless beast that flies by levitating. Falkor, the luckdragon in the novel, is unlike the traditional terrifying dragon. He is an optimist, believing in the power of good luck and perseverance. He tells young Atreyu that if he never gives up, good luck will find him. Even when Falkor is trapped in an enormous web stretched across the Deep Chasm and struggling against a swarm of poisonous insects, he does not give up. Falkor credits Atreyu with helping him escape the web. He carries the boy on his back in search of the Southern Oracle.

Falkor is as talented as he is kind. Despite his enormous size, he is as light as a summer cloud and needs no wings to fly. He can fly while sleeping, fly on his back, and perform perfect loop-the-loops. Falkor whizzes through the mists and shreds of clouds so rapidly that Atreyu gasps for breath. When circling the night sky above the Lake of Tears, Falkor sings a song of pure joy in his bell-like voice, which is so beautiful it opens the heart of every listener.

ACTUAL SIZE

WHERE IN THE WORLD?

FANTASTICA

LAKE OF TEARS

Falkor the luckdragon lives in the land of Fantastica, a place where the geography is ever-changing because it is determined by wishes.

DID YOU KNOW?

- Luckdragons feed on air and heat. They require no other food. Without air and heat, they live only a short time.

- Viewed from the earth, a luckdragon flying overhead resembles a slow flash of lightning or a white flame.

- The rider traveling on the back of a luckdragon experiences a smooth ride despite the great speed of travel.

- As a creature of air and fire, water is the luckdragon's enemy. Water can suffocate or extinguish the flame of a luckdragon because they are always inhaling air.

- Falkor understands the language of water because all the languages of joy are closely related.

Nidhogg

HEIGHT
According to some sources, Nidhogg is taller than a multistory building. It can rear up on its hind legs but walks on all fours.

JAWS
Nidhogg's teeth are sharp and housed in powerful jaws. They ooze with the juice from corpses and tree-root sap.

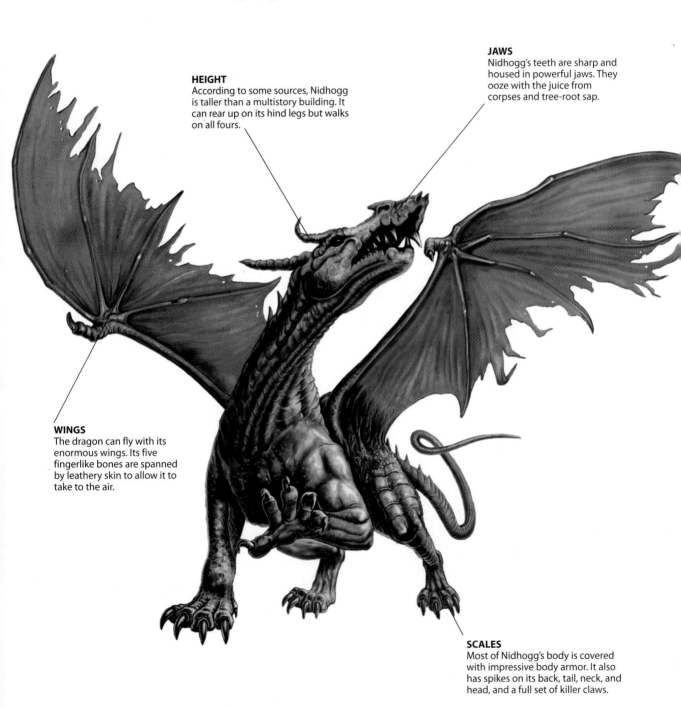

WINGS
The dragon can fly with its enormous wings. Its five fingerlike bones are spanned by leathery skin to allow it to take to the air.

SCALES
Most of Nidhogg's body is covered with impressive body armor. It also has spikes on its back, tail, neck, and head, and a full set of killer claws.

Nidhogg is a mighty dragon from Norse and Germanic legend. It lives in the realm of the dead known as Niflheim or Helheim, and its name means "the tearer of corpses." Nidhogg eats the flesh of dead people, thrown down to it from Earth. It is also known to suck the blood of liars, cheats, and murderers. Nidhogg's home is a pit of venomous serpents near Hvergelmir, or "the bubbling cauldron," a spring that is the source of the world's rivers.

ACTUAL SIZE

As a change from eating dead flesh and drinking blood, Nidhogg sometimes chews at the roots of Yggdrasil, the tree of life. It finally succeeds in gnawing through the roots of the tree, with the help of four serpents, but this sparks a war on Earth. After a dreadful three-year winter, the gods fight the frost giants in a monumental battle at Ragnarok. Nidhogg is involved but is not killed. The dragon survives and returns to its home, where it feasts on the many bodies thrown to it from the battlefield.

WHERE IN THE WORLD?

Tales of Nidhogg encompass myths from many northern European countries, including Germany, Denmark, Sweden, Norway, Iceland, and the Netherlands.

DID YOU KNOW?

• **An eagle lives at the top of the tree of life. Nidhogg sometimes breaks from its meal of corpses to send a squirrel up the tree to torment the eagle.**

• **Nidhogg's name is sometimes said to mean "the dread biter," "striking full of hatred," or "evil blow."**

• **Some stories say that when Nidhogg entered the battle of Ragnarok, it took corpses with it to help with the fighting.**

• **A dragon or monster named Nidhogg appears as a character in several computer and video games, and also in a Viking Lego set.**

Norwegian Ridgeback

BODY
At birth, the scales covering the body are thin and soft. As the dragon matures, they harden into impenetrable plates.

HEAD
Bronze horns are employed to fight other dragons for dominance. During courtship, males use their horns to strip trees of bark and cottages of shingles in order to impress females.

WINGS
Leathery wings help the dragon fly, hunting and swooping down on its unsuspecting prey.

CLAWS
Curved, razor-sharp talons give the dragon a firm, deadly grip as it bears its prey away to kill and devour it in a secluded location.

JAWS
Muscular jaws lined with poisonous fangs are used to kill the water-dwelling creatures and large mammals upon which the dragon feeds. Its intense roar confuses and paralyzes its prey with fear.

Hagrid, keeper of the keys and grounds at Hogwarts, keeps a baby Norwegian Ridgeback named Norbert as a pet in J.K. Rowling's *Harry Potter and the Sorcerer's Stone*. Hagrid wins the black dragon egg from a stranger during a card game and secretly brings it back to Hogwarts. He hatches the egg by placing it in the center of a fire. Within one week, Norbert is three times his original size and smoke is issuing from his nostrils. Norbert sneezes sparks, a sign he will soon develop into a full-fledged fire-breather.

According to *Fantastic Beasts and Where to Find Them* by Newt Scamander, a required text at Hogwarts School, the Norwegian Ridgeback is extremely aggressive to its own kind, making it a rare dragon. Legend states that one carried away and devoured a baby whale off the coast of Norway in 1802. Norbert is a hazard in captivity. He rattles windows when banging his tale against the wall. Wounds from the bite of his poisonous fangs turn green. Hagrid must feed Norbert dead rats by the crate to satisfy his ravenous appetite.

ACTUAL SIZE

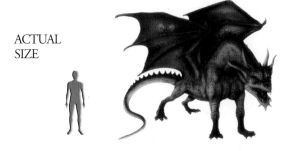

WHERE IN THE WORLD?

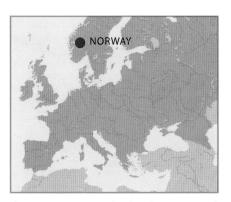

NORWAY

The Norwegian Ridgeback originated in the Norwegian mountains, where it eats water-dwelling creatures and singes the landscape on a regular basis. There have also been sightings at Hogwarts in England and in Romania.

DID YOU KNOW?

• **According to Headmaster Dumbledore, one of the 12 uses of dragon's blood is as oven cleaner.**

• **The Warlock's Convention of 1709 outlawed dragon breeding. It is illegal to keep a dragon as a pet in the wizarding world.**

• **Dragon eggs are considered Class A Non-Tradeable Goods.**

• **Hatchlings should be fed a bucket of chicken blood and brandy.**

• **Despite Hagrid's good intentions, Norwegian Ridgebacks are impossible to train or domesticate.**

• **It is especially unwise to keep a fire-breathing dragon as a pet if you live in a wooden house.**

• **Dragons guard the high-security vaults at Gringotts Wizards Bank, deep beneath London.**

Ryujin

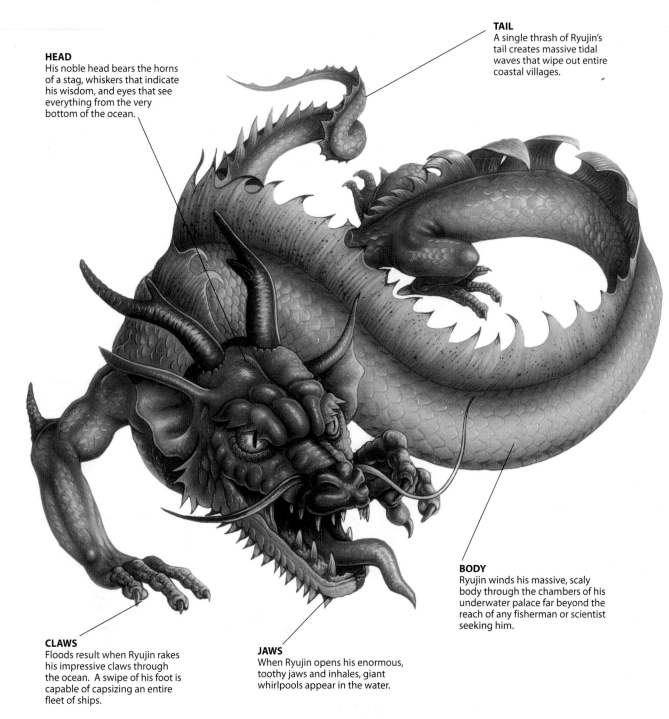

TAIL
A single thrash of Ryujin's tail creates massive tidal waves that wipe out entire coastal villages.

HEAD
His noble head bears the horns of a stag, whiskers that indicate his wisdom, and eyes that see everything from the very bottom of the ocean.

BODY
Ryujin winds his massive, scaly body through the chambers of his underwater palace far beyond the reach of any fisherman or scientist seeking him.

CLAWS
Floods result when Ryujin rakes his impressive claws through the ocean. A swipe of his foot is capable of capsizing an entire fleet of ships.

JAWS
When Ryujin opens his enormous, toothy jaws and inhales, giant whirlpools appear in the water.

In Japanese mythology, Ryujin is the dragon god of the sea. He lives beneath the ocean in a jeweled palace made of red and white coral. His palace has a snowy winter hall, a spring hall where cherry trees grow, a summer hall with chirping crickets, and a fall hall with colorful maple trees. For a human, one day at Ryujin's underwater palace is equal to a hundred years on Earth. Ryujin controls the tides with magical sea jewels. Humans must approach Ryujin carefully because no mortal can glimpse his entire body and survive the sight.

The Empress Jingo asks Ryujin for assistance in the attack she plans against Korea. Ryujin's messenger brings her the two tide jewels. Jingo sails toward Korea with the Japanese fleet. The Korean fleet meets them at sea. Jingo flings the low-tide jewel into the sea and all the waters disappear, stranding the Korean ships. When the Korean soldiers leap from their ships to attack on foot, Jingo casts the high-tide jewel onto the seabed. All the waters rush back, drowning the Korean soldiers.

ACTUAL SIZE

WHERE IN THE WORLD?

JAPAN

Ryujin, the dragon god of the sea, lives at the bottom of the ocean near the Ryukyu Islands, which belong to Japan.

DID YOU KNOW?

• **Ryujin's beautiful daughter married Prince Hoori. This makes Ryujin the ancestor of all the Japanese emperors.**

• **Because Japanese dragons are related to royalty, no one is allowed to harm them. Since they have nothing to fear from humans, Japanese dragons have become tame over the years. Dragons may be seen blocking traffic in cities or sunning themselves on rocks off Japan's shores.**

• **Many dragons are shape shifters. They can change into the form of a human, mate, and produce human offspring.**

• **In both Japan and China, the dragon is one of the guardian animals of the four directions. The dragon guards the eastern compass point and is associated with the season of spring.**

Shen-Lung

BODY
Shen-Lung is a shape shifter who can change his body into human form, stretch from heaven to Earth, or reduce himself to the size of a mouse.

HEAD
Chinese dragons have the head of a camel, eyes of a rabbit, horns of a stag, and ears of a bull.

CLAWS
Tiger paws bear the claws of an eagle. When Shen-Lung rakes his claws across another dragon during a midair fight, storms result.

JAWS
Shen-Lung exhales a breath of clouds that can become fire or rain. He basks in the sun with his whiskered jaws hanging open, hoping that a delicious sparrow will land in his mouth.

In China, Shen-Lung is the spiritual dragon who is responsible for making weather. The right amount of rain is essential for healthy crops, so his power over rain gives Shen-Lung the authority over life and death in China. He must be approached with the utmost respect and reverence. It is important not to offend Shen-Lung, because if he feels neglected, he gets angry. The result is terrible weather in the form of floods or drought, which could destroy the life-giving crops upon which the Chinese depend.

Because of his great power, Shen-Lung grows lazy over the years. He shrinks himself to the size of a mouse in order to hide and avoid work. When lightning strikes a house or tree, it is because the thunder god is sending his servant to search for Shen-Lung. Shen-Lung floats across the sky, his body stretching farther than the eye can see. He is benevolent but bad-tempered. The worst floods in Chinese history were unleashed by Shen-Lung when he was offended by a mortal.

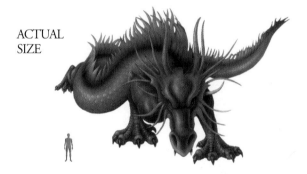

ACTUAL SIZE

WHERE IN THE WORLD?

CHINA

Shen-Lung is the spiritual dragon who has control over the winds and the rains that affect all the crops grown in China.

DID YOU KNOW?

• **Shen-Lung's voice is heard in hurricanes and his claws can be seen in flashes of lightning.**

• **When Shen-Lung is sick, the rain has a distinctly fishy smell.**

• **The dragon is the emblem representing the Chinese emperor, and the phoenix represents the empress. Together, the dragon and the phoenix are used as symbols of marital harmony.**

• **All Chinese dragons have nine distinct features: the head of a camel, scales of a carp, horns of a stag, eyes of a rabbit, ears of a bull, neck of a snake, belly of a clam, paws of a tiger, and claws of an eagle.**

• **The dragon ranks first in the Chinese mythological hierarchy of 360 scaled creatures.**

• **Glass was thought to be solidified dragon breath.**

DRAGONS AND SERPENTS

Smaug

EYES
Blazing eyes emit a thin, piercing red beam that casts a dragon spell.

WINGS
A noise like a roaring wind is produced by the flapping of Smaug's enormous wings.

JAWS
Smaug's fiery breath at full force reduces every building in town to a heap of ashes. He produces a roar that is so fierce and deafening it causes avalanches.

LEGS
Muscular legs trample the ground with power enough to shake the roots of mountains. His claws are capable of crushing boulders.

BODY
Nothing, not a sword, arrow, or curse, can penetrate Smaug's tough hide. His underside is vulnerable but usually covered with treasure.

TAIL
A single sweep of Smaug's mighty tail is all it takes to smash the roof of Esgaroth's Great House.

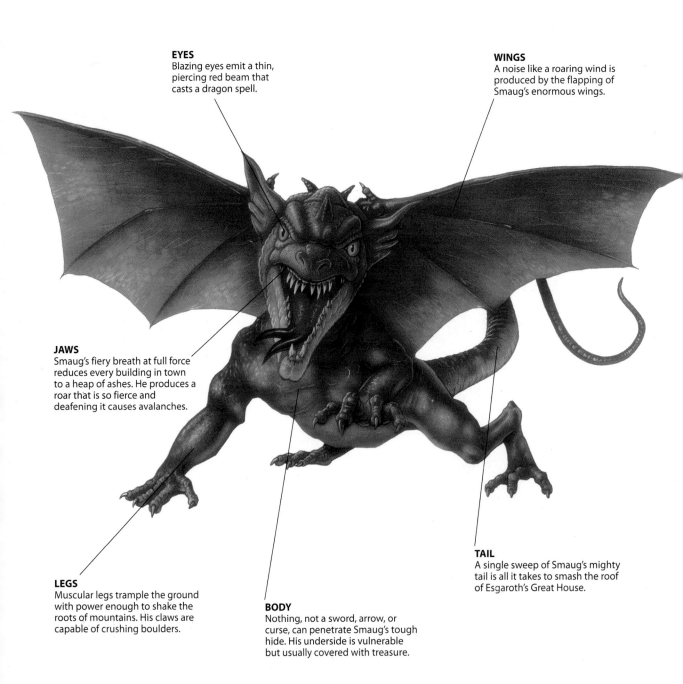

Isolated deep within the Lonely Mountain, Smaug the Golden sleeps atop the pile of treasure that he stole from the dwarves. Smaug makes his bed on the mass of ornaments, utensils, weapons, and gems that he hoards. He lies upon the gems for so long that they stick to his soft belly, forming a dazzling protective armor. At the end of a hot tunnel in a dungeon hall dug by dwarves, Smaug's gurgling snore can be heard. His lair gives off an eerie red glow and wisps of vapor.

Although one of Smaug's drooping eyelids stays open enough to watch for thieves, Bilbo Baggins, a hobbit, is able to sneak in and steal a two-handled cup from the treasure hoard. The discovery of this theft infuriates Smaug. He circles the sky above the mountain in a rage, bellowing and shooting flames. Later, Bilbo makes himself invisible and sneaks into the dragon's cave again. Although Smaug cannot see Bilbo, he can smell him and he mocks the invisible hobbit. Bilbo flatters the vain Smaug into rolling over onto his back. Bilbo spots an open patch in Smaug's jeweled armor. Knowledge of his weak spot is passed on to Bard the Bowman, who kills Smaug with a single, black, dwarf-made arrow.

ACTUAL SIZE

WHERE IN THE WORLD?

LONELY MOUNTAIN

Smaug is the last of the great dragons of Middle-earth in J.R.R. Tolkien's *The Hobbit*. His lair is deep within Lonely Mountain.

DID YOU KNOW?

• It is unwise to reveal one's true name to a dragon.

• Many experts believe that a dragon is able to breathe fire because it stores a mixture of gases in its body. These gases ignite upon contact with the air, producing an intense flame.

• The dragon's ability to store gases such as methane may account for its terrible stench.

• There is no record of any dragon dying of old age. All dragons in recorded history have died from accidents, disease, or battle injuries.

• Dragons have heightened senses of smell, sight, and hearing. Some breeds can see objects as far as a mile (1.6 km) away and hear sounds well out of the range of the human ear.

St. George's Dragon

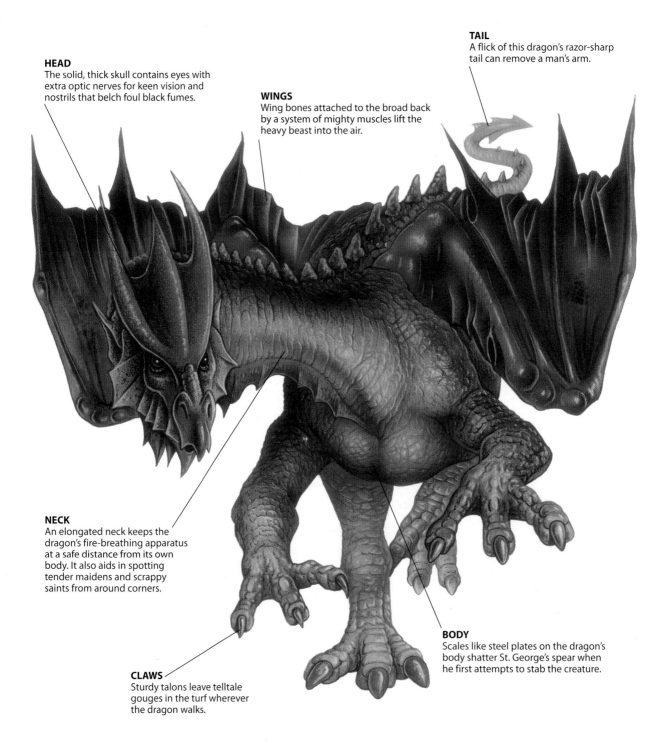

TAIL
A flick of this dragon's razor-sharp tail can remove a man's arm.

HEAD
The solid, thick skull contains eyes with extra optic nerves for keen vision and nostrils that belch foul black fumes.

WINGS
Wing bones attached to the broad back by a system of mighty muscles lift the heavy beast into the air.

NECK
An elongated neck keeps the dragon's fire-breathing apparatus at a safe distance from its own body. It also aids in spotting tender maidens and scrappy saints from around corners.

CLAWS
Sturdy talons leave telltale gouges in the turf wherever the dragon walks.

BODY
Scales like steel plates on the dragon's body shatter St. George's spear when he first attempts to stab the creature.

This bloodthirsty dragon lives by a spring that provides all the water for the city of Cyrene. Whenever the citizens of Cyrene want water, they are faced with the immense beast. Unhappy with the diet of sheep the citizens feed it, the dragon demands human sacrifices. A human sacrifice has to be given to the dragon daily before it allows anyone to draw water from the spring. The only fair way to determine the daily victim is by drawing lots.

ACTUAL SIZE

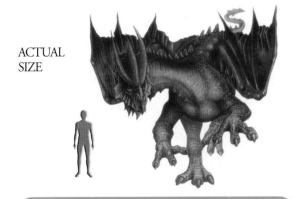

The princess is chosen as the next victim, and her father, the king, is distraught. He offers the citizens all his riches if they will spare his daughter, but the citizens refuse. The princess is tied to a wooden stake. St. George, a soldier of the Roman Empire, discovers the distressed princess and unties her. St. George charges the dragon on horseback. His sturdy lance penetrates deep enough only to wound the creature. Using the princess's sash as a leash, St. George and the princess lead the injured dragon into town. St. George announces he will finish off the dragon if the citizens convert to Christianity. They agree to convert and St. George draws his sword and kills the dragon.

WHERE IN THE WORLD?

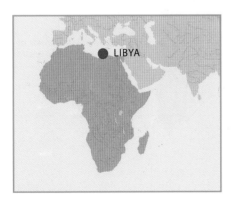

LIBYA

This dragon nests at a spring that provides water for the citizens of Cyrene, Libya, which is situated in northern Africa.

DID YOU KNOW?

• **St. George is the patron saint of England, knights, archers, and butchers.**

• **The flag of Wales bears the image of a red dragon. It is believed to be the oldest national flag still in use.**

• **Hundreds of years ago, dinosaur fossils were believed to be dragon bones.**

• **Dragoon soldiers carried a musket called the dragon. The musket was given this name because it emitted flames when fired.**

• **The various parts of the dragon are believed to have magical properties. Anyone eating dragon's heart will be able to understand the speech of birds. Eating dragon's tongue gives one the power to win any argument. Dragon's blood provides protection against injury from swords.**

DRAGONS AND SERPENTS

Wyvern

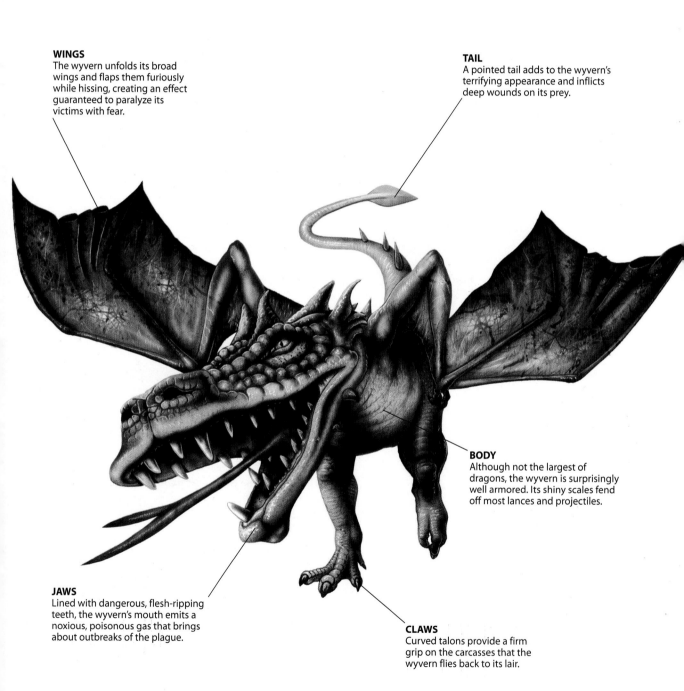

WINGS
The wyvern unfolds its broad wings and flaps them furiously while hissing, creating an effect guaranteed to paralyze its victims with fear.

TAIL
A pointed tail adds to the wyvern's terrifying appearance and inflicts deep wounds on its prey.

BODY
Although not the largest of dragons, the wyvern is surprisingly well armored. Its shiny scales fend off most lances and projectiles.

JAWS
Lined with dangerous, flesh-ripping teeth, the wyvern's mouth emits a noxious, poisonous gas that brings about outbreaks of the plague.

CLAWS
Curved talons provide a firm grip on the carcasses that the wyvern flies back to its lair.

The most famous wyvern is one adopted as a pet by young Maud. While walking in the woods near her home in Mordiford, Maud discovers a baby wyvern. Its body is no bigger than a cucumber and is covered in sparkling, bright-green scales. Maud takes the helpless wyvern home, but her parents forbid her to keep it. Instead of setting it free, Maud hides the tiny dragon. She feeds it milk and plays with it. The wyvern grows rapidly and soon milk is not enough to satisfy its appetite. The wyvern begins to feast on local livestock.

ACTUAL SIZE

WHERE IN THE WORLD?

ENGLAND

In medieval Mordiford, Herefordshire, in England, wyverns were plentiful. It seemed almost anyone could stumble across one with little effort.

The wyvern quickly discovers that farmers make better meals than farm animals. Despite its newly acquired taste for human flesh, the wyvern remains gentle with Maud. Garston, a man from one of Mordiford's best families, dons his armor and rides out to slay the wyvern. Garston's shield protects him from the flame-spouting wyvern. Garston pierces the wyvern's shiny scales with his sword, fatally wounding the creature. Maud kneels on the bloodied grass beside the wyvern. Weeping, she cradles her dying friend in her arms.

DID YOU KNOW?

• Because of their flesh-eating habits, wyverns make unsatisfactory pets. Although they are harmless as babies, a dragon's bloodthirsty instincts always set in when it reaches adulthood.

• The wyvern is associated with war, pestilence, and envy. It is believed to bring outbreaks of the plague wherever it goes.

• Its traits of strength, power, and endurance made the wyvern a popular symbol on medieval coats of arms. Its image on shields was used to strike fear into the hearts of enemies.

• British dragons have been known to inhabit places as diverse as caves, fields, woods, swamps, gullies, moors, corn stacks, water holes, and abbey ruins.

• The coat of arms of Moscow bears the image of a soldier on horseback spearing a wyvern.

Fafnir

Area: Norway

Features: Dragon with leathery wings; scales as strong as iron; poisonous breath; stomach is the weakest part of its body

Futs-Lung

Area: Deep inside the Earth

Features: Dragon can change into any shape it wants or be invisible; bulging eyes; scalloped fin along the length of its back; the pearl of wisdom glows beneath its chin

Gorynych

Area: Russia, Ukraine

Features: Dragon with three heads and seven tails; iron claws; wings; scaly body that smells like sulfur; walks on two hind legs and has two small front legs

Hatuibwari

Area: Solomon Islands, Melanesia

Features: Half human, half snake; wings; four eyes; clawed hands

Hungarian Horntail

Area: Hungary

Features: Dragon with a spike-lined tail; bronze horns; breathes fire; sharp, curved claws; yellow eyes with an extra, reflective layer

Jawzahr

Area: Iran

Features: Dragon with jaws large enough to swallow the sun or moon; claws; huge wings; horned head can live without its body

Jormungand

Area: Midgard, one of nine worlds in Norse myth

Features: Huge snake that eventually grows long enough to encircle the world; dagger-like fangs that hold powerful venom

Knucker

Area: England

Features: Water-dwelling dragon; eel-shaped body; tail can knock down trees; small wings used for low flight and as fins in water; eyes that glow with a chemical allowing it to see across great distances; wide jaws; teeth larger than railroad spikes

Krak's Dragon

Area: Poland

Features: Massive head; long, strong tail; broad wings; hooked claws; breathes fire; pointed fangs

Kraken

Area: Norway

Features: Three-headed sea monster with giant tentacles; huge suckers underneath the tentacles; beak-like mouth

Ladon
Area: Canary Islands
Features: Hundred-headed dragon that never sleeps; thick tail; muscular, serpentine body; each head has a mouth lined with sharp teeth

Lambton Worm
Area: Northumbria
Features: Magical serpent; sharp teeth; jaw has nine holes on each side; if cut into pieces, it can join its parts back together

Luckdragon
Area: Fantastica
Features: A graceful, pearl-colored body; can breathe blue flames; eyes glow; large back to carry riders; flies by levitating

Nidhogg
Area: Niflheim (Helheim)
Features: As tall as a multistory building; powerful jaws with sharp teeth; body armor and spikes on back, tail, neck, and head; huge wings

Norwegian Ridgeback
Area: Norway
Features: Leathery wings; impenetrable scales; bronze horns; razor-sharp talons; poisonous fangs

Ryujin
Area: Japan
Features: Dragon god of the sea; horns of a stag; toothy jaws; long scaly body; his movements cause floods, whirlpools, and waves

Shen-Lung
Area: China
Features: Spiritual dragon who can change into anything, including a mouse; head of a camel, eyes of a rabbit, horns of a stag, ears of a bull; tiger paws have eagle claws; exhales clouds

Smaug the Golden
Area: Deep within the Lonely Mountain
Features: Blazing eyes can cast a spell; enormous wings that sound like a roaring wind when in motion; tough hide; breathes fire; muscular legs

St. George's Dragon
Area: Libya
Features: Solid, thick skull; extra optic nerves for better vision; breathes fire; long neck; scales like steel plates; razor-sharp tail

Wyvern
Area: England
Features: Small-bodied dragon; broad wings; breath brings about disease; dangerous teeth; curved talons; shiny protective scales

Glossary

accommodate: to give something needed

aerodynamic: to move easily through the air

archer: someone who shoots using bows and arrows

benevolent: wanting to do good

convert: to change from one belief to another

culinary: having to do with cooking

deface: to destroy a surface

desperate: without hope

deteriorate: becoming poorer in condition

dorsal: on the upper surface of an animal's body

durable: able to last a long time

extinguish: to stop from burning

gruesome: awful

hoard: to keep many things to oneself

impenetrable: impossible to pass through

infest: to swarm around in a bothersome way

infuriate: to make very angry

malice: meanness

maneuver: a skillful action

medieval: having to do with the Middle Ages

obstruct: to get in the way of sight or movement

paralyze: unable to move

secluded: out of sight

sinister: frightening

unobstructed: not blocked

vulnerable: able to be hurt

For More Information

Books

Ende, Michael. *The Neverending Story.* New York, NY: Dutton Children's Books, 1997.

Green, Jen. *Chinese and Japanese Myths.* New York, NY: Gareth Stevens Publishing, 2010.

McCaughrean, Geraldine. *The Golden Hoard: Myths and Legends of the World.* New York, NY: M. K. McElderry, 1996.

Rowling, J.K. *Fantastic Beasts and Where to Find Them.* New York, NY: Arthur A. Levine Books, 2001.

Troupe, Thomas Kingsley. *The Truth About Dragons.* Mankato, MN: Picture Window Books, 2010.

Web Sites

Folktales from China
www.pitt.edu/~dash/china.html
Read myths and stories from many dragons' homeland.

J.K. Rowling's Official Site
www.jkrowling.com
Learn more about the author of the Harry Potter series.

Saint George and the Dragon
www.nga.gov/kids/rogier/rogier1.htm
See Rogier van der Weyden's paintings about St. George and the dragon in the National Gallery of Art's collection. Try activities about animals as symbols in art.

Publisher's note to educators and parents: Our editors have carefully reviewed these Web sites to ensure that they are suitable for students. Many Web sites change frequently, however, and we cannot guarantee that a site's future contents will continue to meet our high standards of quality and educational value. Be advised that students should be closely supervised whenever they access the Internet.

Index